GW00675824

Alderney

A Little Souvenir

CHRIS ANDREWS PUBLICATIONS LTD

Alderney

West coast and Burhou

Stuart Trought
President of The States of Alderney 2012-

Alderney means many things to many people. Everyone who has ever visited the Island will carry their own unique memories.

Let us not forget our geography and history to both of which we owe much. As the Channel Island nearest to both France and England we have paid allegiance, through the Duke of Normandy, to the English Crown since 1066. This has helped shape our heritage, and our future, allowing us our own government and a remarkable degree of independence.

Alderney today boasts an extraordinarily diverse wealth of fauna, flora, and birdlife, as well as enjoying better weather than the U.K. These together with the stunning scenery and unspoilt beaches make this unchanging gem a haven of tranquility for both visitors and residents alike.

After enjoyable days spent in whatever manner an individual chooses, respite can be found in a wide range of excellent accommodation, bars and restaurants.

Enjoy this small book which will give you a visual insight into Alderney's character. Alderney offers a warm welcome to all, come and see for yourself.

ALDERNEY

Alderney is an attractive island with a distinctive character. Situated some seventy miles to the south of the United Kingdom, but only seven miles off the coast of France, west of Cherbourg and in the English Channel (or *La Manche*). It is the most northerly of The Channel Islands, with Guernsey and Jersey away to the south west.

The Island is three and a half miles long by one and a half wide, the greater part open countryside; its charm is a mixture of the nature of St Anne, the major settlement with ancient cobbled streets and interesting buildings, and the spectacular sea and landscape of the largely unspoilt countryside outside the Town. The south and south-western coasts are

Guernsey cows on Alderney

mainly cliffs up to 270ft high, the northern and eastern coasts are lower and flatter with sandy beaches of varying sizes. There are numerous paths across the Island as well as rewarding cliff walks from which to see some of the 800 species of plants and 260 species of birds recorded here, many of them unique to Alderney or rare on the mainland.

The Island has a nature reserve looked after by The Alderney Wildlife Trust and a golf course in addition to all sorts of other attractions and is popular for walking, angling, birdwatching and sailing as well as traditional beach style

Platte Saline with Fort Tourgis beyond 7

Spring flowers and fields surrounding the Town

10 Fishing boat in the inner harbour

holidays. There are frequent summer events including an air race, fishing competitions and 'Alderney Week', the annual carnival with parties, competitions and parades to suit all tastes.

The main facilities, shops, hotels and restaurants are in the Town, a short steep walk up from the harbour, which as well as being the commercial port for the Island caters for visiting yachtsmen and ferries from France and the other Channel Islands. Visitors may also arrive by air, landing at one of the smallest commercial airports in the British Isles.

Alderney is a thriving community which encourages and welcomes visitors. It has a range of attractions throughout the season and this book attempts to show some of its unique charm.

12   Pretty houses and floral displays in Town

St Anne has many interesting historic houses as well as a variety of shops and restaurants   13

14   Fort Tourgis

The Town church, sometimes known as 'The Cathedral of The Channel Isles'   15

16   The house formerly owned by the famous cricket personality John Arlott

St Anne, Newtown and the Banquage from Braye Bay   17

18 Working fishermen in the inner harbour

20   Gannet Rock

Fisherman at the rocks   21

22   Autumnal view of Braye from the east

East to the Lighthouse

26   Alderney Breakwater and Braye Bay from the Butes

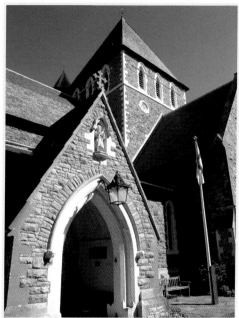

Clock tower of the old town church with the museum entrance, and the present day church   27

28   Fort Albert over Braye Bay

West coast cliffs in the autumn   29

30 Alderney is well known for its wild flowers, which grow abundantly, including in walls

Bluebells and white garlic flowers in spring   31

32   The golf course has spectacular views over much of the Island and surrounding seas

Hoary Stock at Crabby Bay and Fort Grosnez   33

34 Exercise of all types is catered for on Alderney – the football ground above the Arsenal

Once derelict, Fort Quesnard has been brought back to life and is now a private residence 35

36   Platte Saline and Burhou

Sunset over rocks to the west of Fort Grosnez   37

38　Sunrise, France may be closer than you think!

Snow is rare, but here etches the west coast against the sea

Pale sands and sweeping beach at Longis

42   Built in 1912 Blanchard Lighthouse is now automated

44   Disused railway lines on the Breakwater and an important sign inland

Alderney has its own car registrations, some particularly appropriate 45

46   Travel to the Island is often by plane, but adverts at the harbour show the sea route is popular

48 Alderney has been involved in many conflicts, this construction from the First World War

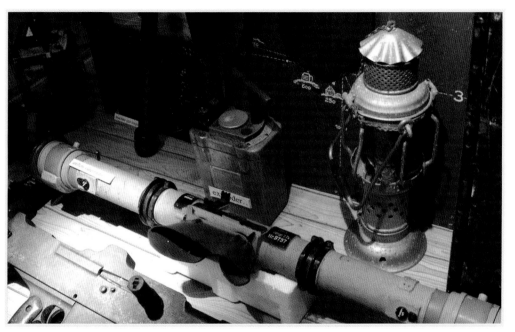

50   The Ile de Raz shows how over the years nature softens the wartime buildings.

Alderney from the north east with the Ile de Raz and Longis Bay   51

52   Nerines are a distinctive Channel Island bloom

Alderney is famous for its natural environment and wildlife, here Small Copper butterflies 53

54   Oystercatcher and the coast from the Ile de Raz

The unique Alderney blonde hedgehog 55

Cliffs and spring flowers on the west coast

57

58 Alderney Week, the annual spectacular celebrations, here the torchlight parade

Alderney week 'Daft Raft' event at Braye   59

60   Fireworks over the cricket ground conclude the Week's activities

A different sort of explosion! winter seas and the Breakwater   61

62   All in all Alderney is probably best known for its wide, safe sandy beaches, ...

Photographed and produced by Chris Andrews Publications

Tel: +44(0)1865 723404 email: chris.andrews1@btclick.com **www: cap-ox.com**

ISBN 978-1-906725-80-8

Grateful thanks to The President, Stuart Trought for kindly contributing the foreword

Photographs by Chris Andrews. Additional material : Ian Laurence, Alderney Wildlife Trust and Joanna Parmentier. Endpaper Maps by David Manby Front Cover: The Island from the south west, Back Cover: Longis Bay, Title Page: Gannets.

Sales of this book help the Alderney Wildlife Trust

This publication has been made possible by the generous support from:

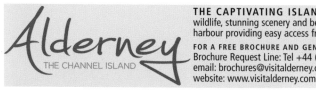